# "NEW MEMBERS OF THE FAMILY"

by: Robert L. Jordan

ISBN: 0-75960-672-2

This book is printed on acid free paper

1stBooks – rev. 2/22/01

As the title of this treatise implies, it is my hope and desire that it's contents may help readers to raise newly-acquired canines into "Kids", who become an integral part of their lives and provide a mutual relationship of companionship, love, contentment and understanding.

My qualifications for this undertaking stem from a life-time of close association with - and study of - such pets. When I was born about eighty years ago, I began life with a family-owned white-haired poodle named Mupsy and I've always had a pet as part of my life.

In recent years, however, developments resulted in the acquisition of two or three at the same time. This change began on Oct. 5,

1982. I retired in 1980 and my wife Marian and I purchased a home in Kings Beach, California, in a remote area north of the main town. Our property backed up to a national forest, which was inhabited by many wild animals, including coyotes, racoons and bears. We had a Cairn terrier named Timothy. At 9:30 a.m. on Oct 5, Timothy went outside by himself. Ten minutes later, when I tried to let him in, Timmy had disappeared. Either he had been stolen from our driveway or animals had carried him away. His loss so shocked and grieved me that I had to visit our doctor. He recommended a replacement for Timmy, as soon as possible. We answered an ad in a Sacramento, California newspaper, offering

Cairn terrier pups for sale. Since Marian and I could not agree on any one puppy, we compromised by purchasing both puppies being considered - a male and a female.

This was a wise decision. We learned to always have two or more such pets at the same time, rather than just one, and I'll discuss this point in detail later on. We named them Katie and Shaughnessy and they became our "New Members of the Family". We lived a full life of joy and contentment with these "Kids" until April 26, 1994, when it became necessary for our veterinarian to put Katie to sleep, after she suffered an incurable old-age illness.

Shaughnessy missed his sister so much that we had to put him in intensive care with

our Vet for awhile. Our Vet advised that Shaughnessy was so lonely, that our only hope for him was to replace Katie as soon as possible. We faced the reality that Shaughnessy was also nearing the end of life. So, if we purchased only one puppy, we would have two "Kids" for only a short time, and then have to purchase another, not related to the remaining one, and quite different in age and background. So, with minimum delay, we purchased our current "New Members of the Family" - male and female Cairn Terrier puppies, now named Paddy and Kelly.

This decision was the right one. Early in 1996, Shaughnessy developed cataracts and lost his eyesight completely. Amazingly,

this did not seem to bother him. He continued his daily routines as always, just as though he had full vision. Then, early in May 1996, his heart and kidneys malfunctioned and we were faced with a no-win situation. The medicine needed to treat his heart adversely affected his kidneys, and vice versa. He deteriorated and finally refused to eat. On May 25, 1996, we sensed from his reactions that he wanted to move on, so I took him to our Vet for his final visit. With his passing, our grief was hard to bear. We'll always remember Katie and Shaughnessy. However, with Kelly and Paddy to fall back on, our grief was less intense and shorter-lived, and we won't have to look back to find happiness and

contentment. We have it with our current "New Members of the Family", now and in the foreseeable future.

Before acquiring Kelly and Paddy, I devoted much time and thought to determine a detailed understanding of the relationship between us and our "Kids". In doing so, I reviewed by relationship with past pets, and with Katie and Shaughnessy, in particular. Based on these experiences, I concluded that there is little spiritual or intellectual difference between us and our "Kids". For reasons of his own, God chose to put us in our human bodies and our pets in their canine bodies. So the major differences between us and our pets are mainly due to the great physical differences in our bodies.

As a result, we each have some advantages and disadvantages over the other. For example, we can talk and our pets can only bark. We have far greater physical mobility and can use our hands in a productive way, while our pets are greatly limited in these aspects by the shape and designs of their front paws. On the other hand, usually our pets have much greater senses of smell, sight and hearing than we do. Mainly because of the physical differences, as we mature we are better able to care for ourselves, carry out decisions we make for our own benefit, and so progress to a better life and greater independence as time goes on. However, in a home environment completely established by us, and with their physical limitations,

our pets can personally satisfy only a small part of their needs and desires, and so must depend on us to service most of the larger portion. Also, I concluded that these "Kids" have the intelligence to realize this situation, prompting them to respond to us in ways which will gain our needed help and support. In addition, it follows that it is always best to have at least two pets as "New Members of the Family", at the same time. In this way, each can interact with the other to provide each with an understanding, companionship, and satisfaction of those needs and desires which are beyond our ability to supply. Also, the frustration of always being totally dependent on us will be assuaged, resulting in a calmer, more

relaxed, and enjoyable life for all. When circumstances require all of us to be away from home at the same time, having two pets left behind will enable each to have the other's companionship to alleviate loneliness and frustration. If there is only one pet left behind, complete loneliness and frustration will ensue. Should these circumstances require kennel boarding for an extended period, two "Kids" can endure this new and traumatic experience together, with less negative results than could one "Kid" facing such a situation alone. In summary, our pets are really persons just as we are, and they and us differ so greatly mainly because we occupy such dissimilar bodies. No two pets

are alike, just as people differ from each other. Each of us-pets included-has his or her own distinctive personality to form a distinctive life pattern.

With these conclusions to guide me, I visited a pet shop in Truckee, California and was advised that two Cairn terrier pups were available from a Kennel in Oregon. If purchased, they would be flown from Medford, Oregon to the Reno, Nevada airport, where they would be picked up by petshop personnel and delivered to me in Truckee, California. One was a female, born April 6, 1994, and the other was a male, born April 10. Apparently, they had the same father and had been together since birth of the youngest. I agreed to the

purchase, with the understanding that our Vet would give each puppy a clean bill-of-health before the purchase was finalized. With my new mind-set resulting from the previously detailed analysis of our relationship with our pets, my concern for the welfare of these puppies had top priority. I realized the extreme trauma each would suffer at their young age, from being enclosed in a small, sealed box while being transported by various means from Medford, Oregon to Truckee, California, then taken to my Vet for a detailed examination and possible vaccinations, and finally taken to my home in Kings Beach, California. To minimize this problem, I determined the earliest possible time I could pick up the

pups at the Truckee pet shop and reserved an appropriate time with our Vet for his examination. I also got his feeding instructions and his recommendations for food for the new "Kids". At the same time, I established with the Vet an appropriate scheduling for the legally required and desirable annual vaccine shots for both "kids" and noted same on my calendar. I also set a date with our Vet for neutering operations for both, since we did not want to breed them and we wanted to relieve them from the stress non-mating could bring as they matured. At the appropriate time these operations were performed. Then I obtained the food from both our pet shop and supermarket, and had it ready at home

before the puppies arrived. If the new "Kids" were to begin acceptance of our house as their new home and start to feel a sense of security, it was necessary that they have a "spot to call their own" in our home, upon their arrival. We have an 8' x 8' entrance hall at our front door, with a linoleum floor - suitable for use for this purpose. I furnished this area with two new pet beds, with appropriate pillows and covers, a water dish and two food dishes, all purchased at our pet shop. I covered the linoleum floor with newspapers for puppy training. There is a stairway from this area to our second floor and another small one leading to our first floor dining room area. I blocked these stairs with collapsible wooden gates, purchased at

our hardware store. This initial living space for the new "Kids" was ready when we brought them home on June 10, 1994, at approximately two months of age.

To minimize the afore-mentioned trauma and to begin showing them we cared, we removed them from the shipping container and Marian carried them on her lap in the car when we left the pet shop and the Vet. When we arrived home, each of us carried one "Kid" into the house, hugging and kissing them all the while. Then, we formally introduced them to Shaughnessy on the living room floor, eventually letting all three sniff each other and become acquainted. Then we gave each new "Kid" a hug and kiss and placed them in their new

home in the entrance hall, giving them some new puppy cookies and water. All of this treatment was to show them that, at long last, the trauma had ended and they were home, were wanted and loved, and had finally started a new and most desirable life ahead.

Next, my concern shifted to Shaughnessy. Being a grown person in his own right, I surmised that he might wonder what was happening, and how he was going to fit into these new developments in our home, with concerns that the new "Kids" might "take-over" and replace him in his relationship with us, now that Katie was gone. It was apparent that a plan of action to develop a

good family relationship with the new "Kids", had to be structured so as to assure Shaughnessy that our relationship with him was unchanged and as bonding as ever, and that the new "Kids" were actually an asset for him, too.

Accordingly, we made certain that our routine handling of Shaughnessy remained unchanged and was not affected in any way by our necessary attention to the new arrivals. We fed him the same food at the same time each day and gave him his special cookies on schedule. I took him outside each day as I had in the past and walked him on schedule. When I reclined in my easy chair to watch television, I continued my practice of cuddling him in my arms or holding him

on my lap, while I stroked his back and gave him an occasional kiss. We continued talking to him at random times, often giving him a hug, pet, and kiss and we responded to his expressed wants and needs, serving his usual needs as always. Our bedroom is on the second floor, reached by the stairs rising from the entrance hall where the new "Kids" were placed. Since Shaughnessy always slept with us on one corner of the foot of our bed, each night at bed-time we opened the two wood gates closing the entrance hall from the rest of the house, and escorted him upstairs to our bedroom. At no time were the new "Kids" allowed upstairs before Shaughnessy passed away. However, as time passed and the "Kids" matured, we

began letting them out of their space in the entrance hall and into our living room for short periods each day, gradually increasing the number and length of these periods as time passed. In this way, Shaughnessy and the new "Kids" began to react positively to each other and establish their own lasting relationship. This strategy and approach was highly successful. It was obvious from Shaughnessy's reaction that he felt completely at ease and still in control. He knew that his relationship with us remained intact and unchanged. He became a father-figure to the new "Kids" and completely accepted their presence in our home - until his time finally came to an end.

Turning now to the matter of raising the "Kids" so that eventually they would become an integral part of our lives in every way, it was apparent to me from my previously detailed analysis of my relationships with past pets, that the first challenge was to establish a mutually workable means of communication with Paddy and Kelly. Pets live an average of 10-12 years, while the life-span of humans is about 70-80 years. So, one year in our new "Kids" lives is equivalent to about seven years for people. Accordingly, this means of communication had to be developed without undue delay, if an entirely satisfactory relationship could be reached by the time the

"Kids" were 6-8 months old, or the equivalent of 3-4 years of age for children.

Since Paddy and Kelly were so greatly dependent on us for satisfaction of their needs and desires, I concluded that their desire for a mutually workable means of communication was also a top priority in their young lives. Yet, their physical ability to outwardly communicate was seriously impaired. They could bark, but not talk. So they had to supplement such expressions with whines, cries, howls, and many different body movements and postures to convey their feelings and messages to us. Based on my past experience with pets, I was certain that even though they couldn't talk, they would eventually understand what

we said to them. So we talked to them at every opportunity, expressing our feelings by the tone and inflection of our voices. We also supplemented our verbal expressions by appropriate bodily movements, such as petting, kissing and even a light slap on the rump when appropriate to convey our reactions to what they had or had not done. A most important part of establishing this communication system was our learning, understanding, and correctly interpreting their verbal expressions and body language, and relating same to their needs and desires. All of these efforts proved highly successful and we now mutually communicate with no apparent problems.

The next step we faced, was to use our system of communication to teach Paddy and Kelly what was right and what was wrong, what they could and could not do in their every day lives, and to do so in such a way that their positive feelings for us continued to grow as they matured. Since they have marked differences in their personalities, their needs and desires are different in many respects, and their individual reactions to events and situations vary considerably. Also, Kelly needs more attention of all kinds than Paddy. So, we had to develop a separate teaching pattern and method for each one. Above all, we did not want the results of this teaching to negatively affect their lives or their

personalities, and thus detract from their individual happiness and contentment. This required that, after a thorough analysis of their individual personalities, needs, and desires, we altered our pre-conceived ideas of what we considered right and wrong and what they could be permitted to do or not do. The net result was a teaching pattern for each new "Kid" that was an acceptable compromise of all our desires, but which still accomplished our basic objectives. I filled the foot-section of an old sock with small gravel pellets and tied a knot in the leg portion. When we failed to get their attention, we threw this gadget on the floor close to them. This got their attention immediately - they stopped what they were

doing - and eased the teaching process. When they committed an unacceptable wrong, we never spanked them. Usually, we lightly held the loose skin on the back of the neck, while we scolded them and focussed their attention on their mistake. Then we released them and left them to contemplate their actions and the results. After a few minutes, we always returned to pet them, kiss their cheek, and give them a small piece of doggie cookie. This scenario got our point across and assured them that their mistake did not alter our positive relationship. Now, whenever they respond positively to our directions or commands we praise them verbally and physically.

Finally, we all cooperate to implement a system of routines, designed to serve the "Kids" needs and desires, and constantly assure them that they are "New Members of the Family". Following our Vet's advice, the "Kids" are fed only one complete meal each day, shortly after get-up time, consisting of food recommended by our Vet and purchased at our pet shop and supermarket. While we are eating our three daily meals, I feed them small pieces of doggie biscuits (purchased at our pet shop), so that each receives one doggie biscuit at each such meal. Each day, for personal health reasons, I eat a handful of shelled peanuts and I share a few nuts with each "Kid". Usually, I conclude my evening meal with ice cream,

and always let Paddy lick the bowl, while Kelly eats a small quantity from the teaspoon. Since our property is not fenced in, I take them outside on the leash for defecation and urination purposes at regular times each day, concluding at 6:00 p.m. If they defecate or urinate, they get a small piece of doggie cookie and a pat on the head when we re-enter the house. Interestingly, if I become involved in some activity and forget the take-out time, they can read the clock. For needed exercise, I walk them with leashes three days each week. On Tuesdays and Thursdays, we walk several blocks up and down our street. On Sunday, we hike about one mile through the national forest behind our house on an asphalt bike trail.

When we have to leave them alone, we make certain all doors are locked, their water bowls are filled, and the radio is tuned to a music station. I take them outside for a few minutes just before we leave. We display our love for them at random times, throughout the day, by petting, hugging and kissing them on the cheek, while verbally expressing our sentiments, and always our favors are copiously returned. As soon as the "Kids" received their first rabies vaccine and collar tags from our Vet - as required by County law - I obtained a County license tag for each from our County animal control center, and an identification tag for each from our hardware store, showing the "Kid" name, our name and address, and phone

number. These three tags were secured to a new collar purchased at our pet store - a red one for Paddy and a blue one for Kelly, so we could easily tell them apart in the house. Each began wearing their collar when I started taking them outside on leashes. As they matured, new collars had to be bought several times to accommodate neck enlargement. Routinely, of course, rabies vaccinations and new licenses are an annual event. Once every two weeks, I clip their toe nails, with an appropriate clipper purchased at our pet shop, and I have a jar of styptic powder (also from our pet shop) readily available to stop bleeding, if a nail is inadvertently cut too short. They really resist this clipping and are so happy when it ends.

Every three months, I take them to our local pet "beauty parlor" for a bath and haircut. Oddly enough, from their reactions and the shop owner's comments, they thoroughly enjoy this visit, probably because of the excitement they realize from being together with other pets at the shop, and because they feel better with clean bodies and hair. We learned that it is most important that these routines be administered equally to each "Kid". Paddy and Kelly have their own routines to serve their needs and desires, as well as ours. Whenever I relax in my easy chair to watch TV, invariably Paddy will sit alongside the chair so I can scratch his head and back, while Kelly jumps up on my lap and covers my face with kisses before she

lies down on the foot stool between my legs and goes to sleep, with her head draped across my left shin. When I sit on the living room sofa to read, Kelly lies next to me and falls asleep and Paddy naps against the sofa below my legs. Whenever either of us leave home for a short time, when we return and start to enter our driveway, both "Kids" frantically bark inside the front door. When we enter, they whine and cry until we bend down and allow them to kiss our cheeks and welcome us home. Whenever I sit down to work at a table, one or both will lie beside my chair. Our living room is fronted by a large sliding glass door and a large sliding glass window to provide a view of the national forest and entrance to our large

outdoor deck. In the living room a large padded window seat lines the entire bottom of the window. For about eight months each year weather permits us to furnish this deck with outdoor furniture, including two padded lounge chairs. At one end of the indoor window seat, we keep shallow 1' x 1' open cardboard box filled with small balls, chew toys and hard-boiled pieces of beef socket bones, purchased at our market. Routinely, every morning, both "Kids" will choose a piece from this box, to play with during the day.

In addition to these routine activities, it is essential that they have plenty of time each day to do their own thing and interact with each other. Often, they play their own game,

suddenly chasing each other around the first floor of our house, while barking, whining and otherwise expressing their fervor. Intermittently, one catches the other and they wrestle on the floor until one breaks away and the chase starts again. Weather permitting, we leave the sliding door to the deck ajar during the day, providing space for the "Kids" to pass through. Quite often, forest squirrels purposely run along the deck railings to "bug" Paddy and Kelly. When they appear, our "Kids" quietly creep to the door on their bellies, watch the squirrels for a time and then burst onto the deck, barking to chase them away. On summer afternoons, both "Kids" often sun bathe on the deck

lounge chairs and take a nap. A quilted blanket covers the padded window seat in our living room and another such blanket covers the seats on our sofa. Often Kelly will choose either place for a nap, first using her mouth and front paws to rearrange the blanket to provide the most comfortable spot and headrest. Most afternoons, Kelly and Paddy will be side by side on the window seat for an hour or so, while looking at birds and squirrels in the forest trees. Paddy's favorite place to nap is on top of the back of an overstuffed chair in our living room, which we keep covered with part of an old blanket.

Of course, all the previously-described activities of our "Kids" in our living room

and on our deck began after they were "housebroken" and while Shaughnessy was still with us. At that time, Shaughnessy accepted their antics without question and quite often, participated in them, indicating that we were able to keep him feeling his old self and confident of his long-established position in our home. When Shaughnessy left us on May 25, 1996, Kelly and Paddy were just two years old, and had been sharing their life with Shaughnessy for the preceeding year or so. During that time, however, they were never permitted to go upstairs, as previously stated, and Shaughnessy maintained this major and singular advantage to assure him of his predominance with us. No doubt, they were

well aware that I came back from the Vet alone the day Shaughnessy died, after leaving the house with him, and they missed him. Our grief was intense and prolonged as we counted each day that passed, while remembering all the details of our lives together - many tears were shed. Shaughnessy's spot on the foot of our bed became a revered place and somehow we felt that he was still there, night after night. Finally, however, Kelly and Paddy brought us back to reality. After several months passed, they began to cry and bark occasionally during the night and Kelly gnawed through several bottom slats on the wood gate, blocking the stairs to our bedroom. Finally, we realized that free

access to this room was the remaining thing they needed before they felt their acceptance as "New Members of the Family" was complete. So, I opened the gate and they raced upstairs, explored the area and spent considerable time examining our bed. That night when we retired, they accompanied us and layed down on the bed while we prepared for the night. The excitement generated by being allowed upstairs for the first time, greatly offset any concern they had for Shaughnessy's absence and being able to sleep with us each night from then on, minimized any grief they might have suffered by his loss. Most importantly, it was Paddy and Kelly who put us back on track to start on our way to the life we all

now enjoy - a major reason for always having at least two "New Members of the Family". Paddy occupies Shaughnessy's old spot, while Kelly sleeps in Katie's place. Before going to these spots, they often cuddle with us while we are watching our last TV show of the day on our bedroom set. Just as though he can read our bedroom clock, almost every morning Paddy wakes us up within five minutes of our usual get-up time, by moving around on the bed.

Quite obviously, we have had considerable success in our handling of Shaughnessy's last few years and preparing the "New Members of the Family" and ourselves for complete enjoyment of our lives ahead, in a home filled to the brim with

companionship, love, contentment, understanding and fond, wonderful memories of days gone by. Marian and I now focus on the past with much happiness and great thanks to Katie and Shaughnessy for all they brought to our past lives, and we face each new day with a complete sense of anticipation and enjoyment.

In closing I would like to point out that we and our bodies are two separate and distinct things. We live in a physical world, so God has given us a body to occupy that is so designed to provide the physical ability and function to do the necessary things to get along in this physical world. As time goes by our bodies wear out from overuse

and finally can no longer do those things necessary for continued existence in this world. So, God takes us from our bodies into a completely spiritual world where bodies are no longer needed for existence and happiness.

Our "New Members of the Family" have the same experience. However, our bodies - on average - last about 7 times as long as theirs. So, we usually have many such "Members of the Family" in our life-time. When it is necessary for them to enter the spiritual world, in my opinion they remain with us as always, waiting for the time when our bodies finally wear out, and we join them spiritually for eternity.

So, when a "Member of the Family" must leave his body, we should not be sad. Instead, we should be glad that God has done what is best for that "Member" at the right time. We should not say goodbye. Instead, "I Love You" and "We'll be together again" would be most appropriate.

As I said previously, when Shaughnessy passed on we were shocked, grieved, and cried. However, since he was enjoying a much better existence in his new spiritual world, our grief was for us and not for him. We cried because we no longer had his body that we could see, pet, and love, although we knew he could still see us as always from his vantage point. But our grief was less intense and assuaged more quickly, because we

already had two "New Members of the Family" to turn to.

We hope this treatise may help readers to successfully raise their "New Members of the Family" and make a convincing case for always having at least two "Kids" at the same time.

# "NOTES"

# "NOTES"

"NOTES"

# "NOTES"

# "NOTES"

# "NOTES"

# "NOTES"

"NOTES"

# "NOTES"

# "NOTES"

"NOTES"

# ABOUT THE AUTHOR

I was born in 1918 in St. Louis, MO. In 1925, I was spanked 5 times by Charles Lindberg for climbing on his plane in a family friend's barn adjacent to the St. Louis airport. In 1939, I received a B.S.E.E. degree from Washington University in St. Louis. In 1942, I joined General Electric Co. as a refrigeration engineer. During W.W. II I was an engineer on the remotely-controlled armament systems for the B29, A26 and P61 military planes, and participated in the first trial flights for the B29 and A26. After WW II, I held GE positions in appliance engineering and marketing,factory employee and community relations at several GE plants. I have lived in or visited all 48 continental US states. I ended my 38 year career in 1980 as Manager-GE Public Affairs Operations in Sacramento, CA. Since then, my wife Marian and I have lived in our own home in Kings Beach, CA, at the north end of Lake Tahoe, with our two Cairn terriers.

In the mid 1950s, I worked for GE in New York City, and sang for many nights over those years in a supper club. As a result, I knew many famous people, including Estelle Winwood, Marlene Dietrich, Tallulah Bankhead, Arthur Godfrey, Aristotle Onassis, Artie Shaw, Frank Parker, Jeannette Forman, Marian Marlowe, Maxene Andrews and the McGuire Sisters. From 1955 until he became President, Ronald Reagan and I were always crossing paths and we spent much personal time together as friends. I have photos taken with him and letters and notes he sent to me. So it's been a full and interesting life, greatly enhanced by always having at least 2 "New Members of the Family" in recent years!

www.ingramcontent.com/pod-product-compliance
Ingram Content Group UK Ltd.
Pitfield, Milton Keynes, MK11 3LW, UK
UKHW040018200726
13854UKWH00001B/255

9 780759 606722